GU00836572

MASONRY AND ITS SYMBOLS

BOOKS by HAROLD W. PERCIVAL

THINKING AND DESTINY

Deluxe One Vol. hardcover edition, complete
Libr. of Congress 47-1811
ISBN: 0-911650-09-1

Quality Softcover edition, complete
Libr. of Congress 47-1811
ISBN: 0-911650-06-7

MASONRY AND ITS SYMBOLS
In the Light of Thinking and Destiny
Libr. of Congress 52-2237
ISBN: 0-911650-07-5

MAN AND WOMAN AND CHILD
Libr. of Congress 52-6126
ISBN: 0-911650-08-3

DEMOCRACY IS SELF-GOVERNMENT
Libr. of Congress 52-30629
ISBN: 0-911650-05-9

Available at your local bookstore, or from:
THE WORD FOUNDATION, INC.
P.O. Box 18235
Dallas, Texas 75218

MASONRY
AND
ITS SYMBOLS

In the Light of
Thinking and Destiny

By
HAROLD WALDWIN PERCIVAL

THE WORD FOUNDATION, INC.

P.O. Box 18235 • Dallas, Texas 75218

Copyright, 1952, by
Harold W. Percival
and
The Word Foundation, Inc.

Copyright, 1980, by
The Word Foundation, Inc.

All rights reserved, including the right to
reproduce this book or portions thereof in
any form.

First Edition, 1952
Second Edition, 1966
Third Edition, 1974
Fourth Edition, 1979
Fifth Edition, 1983

ISBN 0-911650-07-5
Library of Congress Catalog Card Number: 52-2237

Printed in the U.S.A.
by
Taylor Publishing Company
Dallas, Texas

DEDICATION

Dedicated with Love to the Conscious Self in every Mason with the hope that this book will help all Masons to get more Light through their symbols.

"Masonry is a worship; but one in which all civilized men can unite; for it does not undertake to explain or dogmatically to settle those great mysteries, that are above the feeble comprehension of our human intellect. It trusts in God, and HOPES; it BELIEVES, like a child, and is humble. It draws no sword to compel others to adopt its belief, or to be happy with its hopes. And it WAITS with patience to understand the mysteries of Nature and Nature's God hereafter."

Albert Pike, *Morals and Dogma*

CONTENTS

FOREWORD

GREETINGS, to all Members of Ancient Free and Accepted Masonry Throughout the World:

Every Mason understands that his advancement through degrees in Masonry is a journey in search of "more Light" — or a quest for knowledge and truth. Masonic degrees, their meaning and ritual of conferment, are deeply steeped in symbolism which transcends all language barriers; therefore the universal appeal of Masonry for thousands of years. Masons also know that rituals and ceremonial badges are meaningless unless each Brother lives according to the obligations he has so solemnly assumed. By understanding the meaning of the symbols, all Masons — and anyone else — will come to see these symbols as guideposts on our road of life as we seek to find our way back to The Realm of Permanence whence we came.

Masonry and Its Symbols, more than any other book known to the Fraternity, provides a link between the esoteric meanings of Ancient Masonry to the more familiar exoteric meanings of today. It will enhance every Mason's likelihood of finding "more Light."

I have been privileged to be a member of the Fraternity for 37 years and a student of this book for 23 of those years. To my Brothers, I sincerely recommend *Masonry and Its Symbols* as priority reading to augment your complete understanding of Masonry.

Dallas, Texas
September, 1983

C. F. Cope
Master Mason

MASONRY AND ITS SYMBOLS

In the Light of *Thinking and Destiny*

By H. W. Percival

PREFACE

T HE SUBJECT MATTER of this little book was originally one of fifteen chapters of a manuscript entitled *Thinking and Destiny,* the publication of which was delayed owing to the paper situation during the Second World War. As time went on it was deemed advisable to delete this chapter from the manuscript, and to publish it at some future time under separate cover and with the assurance that it would not be disapproved by the Masonic Fraternity. It is now published on the suggestion of Masons who have read the manuscript.

In order to understand this book, it is necessary to be somewhat familiar with a few terms and general ideas advanced in *Thinking and Destiny.* That book deals generally with the entirety of the universe beyond the reach or range of human thought, but chiefly with mankind. It tells about the long-forgotten past of the present human being; about that life in a perfect, sexless, physical body (the "first temple") in The Realm of Permanence; about the need of undergoing a trial and test of the sexes, and about the failure of the "Doer" in that perfect body to pass that test. Thereby was brought about the "fall of man" and his exile into this imperfect sexual world in which man finds himself now. The book tells further that each human will in some life free himself from this unbalanced world; that is, he must regenerate his human imperfect body and rebuild for himself another, perfect, sexless, immortal physical body, — the "second temple" of Masonry. In that "house not made with hands, eternal in the heavens," the Doer then takes up again and continues the work which was left unfinished, and goes on — in The Eternal Order of Progression — in being conscious in ever higher degrees of being conscious.

New and valuable information is given in *Thinking and Destiny* on such subjects as: Destiny; Re-existence; what the "soul" is; about The Government of the human world, and Triune Selves and the administrators of the law; about The Great Way, which is The Path on which the progress of the Doer in man proceeds while he is rebuilding that perfect, immortal physical body.

The reader should understand that what in him is his conscious self is "feeling-and-desire," which is only a small fraction of the inseparable Doer part of a trinity, termed in the book the "Triune Self"; the other two parts of the Triune Self are the "Thinker-Knower," who is the Doer's "Lord God."

Feeling, commonly spoken of as one of five senses, is not a sense at all, because feeling is part of the conscious self, the Doer of feeling-desire, and does not belong to nature. There are only the four senses of sight, hearing, taste and smell, and these do belong to nature.

"Breath-form" is another term that should be understood. The breath-form is the "trestle board" of the Mason. The form part of the breath-form unit is what has been spoken of as the "soul"; it is somewhat like a screen upon which are inscribed the Doer's thoughts and deeds and the events of his life. With the first gasp of the infant at birth, the breath unites with the "form" in the body as the breath-form, the so-called "living soul." It continues to build out the structure of the body according to the form's pattern.

There is that which in the human relates the intelligent-side of the universe on which the Triune Self is, with the nature-side on which the breath-form is — here spoken of as the "aia." It serves as an intermediary between the Doer and the breath-form.

To anticipate one difficulty which the reader is liable to have, namely, to understand how the author could possibly know about the things of which he speaks, — it should be explained that *Thinking and Destiny* was written in an unusual manner — not through revelation, not in trance, not by automatic writing, but through hard, persistent thinking according to a certain system which is explained in that book. In his Foreword the author tells something of the way he wrote the book. For the readers of "MASONRY, and its Symbols, in the Light of *Thinking and Destiny,*" the following extracts are here given:

"Thoughtful persons have stressed the need of speaking here of some of my experiences in states of being conscious, and of events of my life which might help to explain how it was possible for me to be acquainted with and to know of things that are so at variance with present beliefs. They say this is necessary because no bibliography is appended and no references are offered to substantiate the statements herein made. Some of my experiences have been unlike anything I have heard of or read. My own thinking about human life and the world we live in has revealed to me subjects and phenomena I have not found mentioned in books. But it would be unreasonable to suppose that such matters could be, yet be unknown to others. There must be those who know but cannot tell. I am under no pledge of secrecy. I belong to no organization of any kind. I break no faith in telling what I have found by thinking, by steady thinking while awake, not in sleep or in trance . . .

"(While a small child) I realized that I was in a body from which I could not free myself. I was lost, alone, and in a sorry state of sadness . . . I could not help being observant of events. What I heard people say about things that happened, particularly about death, did not seem reasonable. My parents were devout Christians. I heard it read and said that 'God' made the world; that He created an immortal soul for each human body in the world; and that the soul who did not obey God would be cast into hell and would burn in fire and brimstone for ever and ever. I did not believe a word of that. It seemed too absurd for me to suppose or believe that any God or being could have made the world or have created me for the body in which I lived . . .

"From November of 1892 I passed through astonishing and crucial experiences, following which, in the Spring of 1893, there occurred the most extraordinary event of my life. I had crossed 14th Street at Fourth Avenue, in New York City. Cars and people were hurrying by. While stepping up to the North East corner curbstone, Light, greater than that of myriads of suns opened in the center of my head. In that instant or point, eternities were apprehended. There was no time. Distance and dimensions were not in evidence. Nature was composed of units. I was conscious of the units of nature and of units as Intelligences. Within and beyond, so to say, there were greater and lesser Lights, which revealed the different kinds of units. The Lights were not of nature, they were Lights as Intelligences, Conscious Lights. Compared with the brightness or lightness of those Lights, the surrounding sunlight was a dense fog. And in and through all Lights and units and objects I was conscious of the Presence of CONSCIOUSNESS. I was conscious of CONSCIOUSNESS as the ULTIMATE and ABSOLUTE REALITY, and conscious of the relation of things. I experienced no thrills, emotions, or ecstasy. Words fail utterly to describe or explain CONSCIOUSNESS. It would be futile to attempt description of the sublime grandeur and power and order and relation in poise of what I was then conscious. Twice during the next fourteen years, for a long time on each occasion, I was conscious of CONSCIOUSNESS. But during that time I was conscious of no more than I had been conscious of in that first moment . . .

"The great worth in being conscious of CONSCIOUSNESS is that it enables one to know about any subject, by thinking. Thinking is the steady holding of the Conscious Light within on the subject of the thinking. Briefly stated, thinking is of four stages: selecting the subject; holding the Conscious Light on that subject; focussing the Light; and, the focus of the Light. When the Light is focussed, the subject is known. By this method, *Thinking and Destiny* has been written.

"The special purpose of this book is: To tell the conscious selves in human bodies that we are inseparable Doer parts of consciously immortal *individual* trinities, Triune Selves, who, within and beyond time, lived with our great Thinker and Knower parts in perfect sexless bodies in The Realm of Permanence; that we, the conscious selves now in human bodies, failed in a crucial test, and thereby exiled ourselves from that Realm of Permanence into this temporal man and woman world of birth and death and re-existence; that we have no memory of this because we put ourselves into a self-hypnotic sleep, to dream; that we will continue to dream through life, through death and back again to life; that we must continue to do this until we de-hypnotize, wake, ourselves out of the hypnosis into which we put ourselves; that, however long it takes, we must awake from our dream, become conscious *of* ourselves *as* ourselves in our bodies, and then regenerate and restore our bodies to everlasting life in our home — The Realm of Permanence from which we came —

which permeates this world of ours, but is not seen by mortal eyes. Then we will consciously take our places and continue our parts in The Eternal Order of Progression."

With an understanding of the above points the reader of "MASONRY and Its Symbols, in the Light of *Thinking and Destiny*" should have no difficulty in intelligently following the text of this book.

THE AUTHOR.

New York City,
December 1, 1951.

LEGEND TO SYMBOLS

Masonic Lodges: Entered Apprentice, Fellowcraft, Master Mason, and Royal Arch degrees, showing the stations or gates of Cancer (♋) the senior warden in the West; Libra (♎) the junior warden in the South; and Capricorn (♑) the master in the East; in each of the degrees. The physical body of man is the ground floor or plan or lodge in which all the degrees are worked, as the body or lodge is prepared for each degree.

The conscious self, as the Doer-in-the-body, is the entered apprentice to be initiated in the first degree. He begins to learn the use of his rule, or line of feeling, from Cancer to Libra (♋ to ♎) and his line of desire from Libra to Capricorn (♎ to ♑). When he has brought these into right relationship to each other they unite and make the square on which a Mason works, and the oblong square (♋ to ♎ to ♑) below. The feeling line and desire line make the square of the right-angled triangle (the hypotenuse), the square of all true Masons on which the work of the lodge is conducted.

All degrees are degrees to be taken by the Doer-in-the-body; not by the Thinker and Knower. They await the Doer on his initiation as a Master Mason. The Doer is initiated into the higher degrees to be eventually united with the Thinker and Knower in the Royal Arch. Then they will be complete and perfect. The work of the Doer as entered apprentice is, as he advances by degrees, to rebuild his present physical body into that temple not made with hands, immortal in The Eternal.

This figure shows the Masonic Lodge to be the present physical body. The oblong square is given in detail. The two columns and the three pillars are, by extension, also shown.

The Groundfloor is the pelvic section. The Middle Chamber is the abdominal section. The Sanctum Sanctorum is the thoracic section. The Royal Arch is the physical body in its atmospheres, complete. The top of the head represents the keystone.

Refer to symbols, pages 945, 960, 961, in *Thinking and Destiny*. On page 961, Fig. VI-B shows the front, or nature, column of the perfect body — which is now broken, being absent below the sternum.

The three signs Cancer, Leo, Virgo (♋ , ♌ , ♍) are the three female signs, from the breasts to the womb; when squared, 3 x 3, they make 9. The male signs are four, Libra, Scorpio, Sagittary, Capricorn (♎ , ♏ , ♐ , ♑), from the coccyx Libra to Capricorn opposite the heart. When squared they equal 16. 9 plus 16 equal 25. The five signs, Aquarius (♒), Pisces (♓), Aries (♈), Taurus (♉), Gemini (♊), are signs representing the hypotenuse, above Cancer (♋) and Capricorn (♑) which when squared equal 25, the square of the circle, thus "squaring the circle."

THE AUTHOR.

New York City,
December 1, 1951.

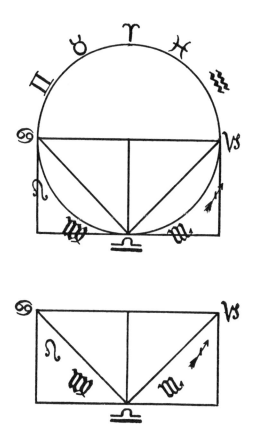

THE OBLONG SQUARE

The lower section is set apart to show the Oblong Square itself. The first three signs, Cancer, Leo, Virgo, are feminine and the next four, Libra, Scorpio, Sagittary, Capricorn, are masculine. The sum of the squares of the first three and the next four is equal to the square of the hypotenuse which, itself, is actually equal to five and conforms to the five unmanifested signs representing the Royal Arch. As is readily seen in the plate, the hypotenuse is equal to one side of the square capable of encompassing the circle. It is the total sum of the Mason's work on the Oblong Square, the trestle board, his lodge, his body, which squares the circle and enables him to take his rightful place as the Keystone in The Royal Arch in The Realm of Permanence.

MASONRY AND ITS SYMBOLS

SECTION 1

The Brotherhood of Freemasons. Compass. Membership. Age. Temples. Intelligences behind Masonry. Purpose and plan. Masonry and religions. The essential and the temporary teachings. The fundamental principles of the three degrees. Offshoots. Great truths locked up in trivial forms. The secret language. Passive and active thinking. Lines on the breath-form. Discipline of desires and of mental operations. The ancient landmarks. Masons should see the importance of their Order.

THE Brotherhood of Freemasons is the largest of the bodies in the world which are outposts to prepare possible candidates for an inward life. They are men drawn from all ranks and races for whose character and intelligence a Master Mason has at one time vouched. Masonry is for Humanity, the conscious self in every human body, not for any special race, religion or clique.

The Order existed under one name or another as a compact, well-organized body long before the building of the oldest pyramid. It is older than any religion known today. It is the extraordinary thing among organizations in the world. This organization and the system of its teachings, with the tools, landmarks, emblems and symbols, have always been substantially the same. It goes back to the age when bodies became male or female. The temple has always been a symbol of a rebuilt human body. Some of the legendary masonic temples, whose place is now taken by that of Solomon, were circles, ovals, squares and oblongs of stones. Sometimes the stones were connected at the top by slabs, later by two pieces of stone pitted against each other in triangular form, and then by semicircular arches. Sometimes the temples were enclosed by walls; these temples were open at the top, and the vault of heaven was the roof. So symbolic temples were built for the worship of the Lord, until the last that figures in the Masonic ritual is called Solomon's Temple.

Intelligences in the earth sphere are behind Masonry, though the lodges are not aware of this in the present age. The spirit that runs through the system of the masonic teachings connect these Intelligences with every Mason, from the greatest to the least, who practices them.

The purpose of Masonry is to train a human being so that he will reconstruct, through the body of change and death which he now has, a perfect physical body which shall not be subject to death. The plan is to build this deathless body, called by modern Masons Solomon's Temple, out of material in the physical body, which is called the ruins of Solomon's Temple. The plan is to build a temple not made with hands, eternal in the heavens, which is the cryptic name for the deathless physical vesture. The Masons say that in the building of Solomon's Temple there was not heard the sound of an axe, hammer or any tool of iron; nor will any sound be heard in the rebuilding of the temple. A Masonic prayer is: "And since sin has destroyed within us the first temple of purity and innocence, may thy heavenly grace guide and assist us in rebuilding a second temple of reformation, and may the glory of this latter house be greater than the glory of the former."

There are no better and no more advanced teachings available to human beings, than those of Masonry. The symbols used in the Craft are chiefly tools of a mason and instruments of an architect. The symbols have been substantially the same from immemorial times; though their shape and interpretation have changed, and though the rituals and lectures about them changed with the prevailing cyclic religion of the age. The doctrines of all religions are so made that they can be used for masonic teachings. In modern western Masonry, that is, what the Masons call Ancient Masonry, Masonry is given in forms of the Hebrew religion, with some additions from the New Testament. The teachings are not Hebrew. But Masonry uses parts of Hebrew traditions to clothe and present its own teachings, because the Hebrew traditions are familiar and acceptable as parts of the Bible. The masonic teachings might be presented in Egyptian or pre-Egyptian Greek clothes, if the people were familiar with them. The Hebrew traditions are colorful and impressive. Besides, the physical body in which the reconstruction has to go on is the divided name of Jahveh or Jah-hovah. Yet the rituals are sometimes easily shaped to exemplify Christianity, by making Christ the Supreme Grand Master, and the Great Architect of the Universe can be interpreted as a Christian God. But Masonry is not Christian any more than it is Jewish. The

temporary interpretations according to age and place and
religion are looked upon by the common run of Masons
as absolute and as the truth.

Often the symbology is obscured by adornments,
additions, changes and omissions. Sometimes whole
Orders are instituted in these ways and specialize a
particular religious, warlike, or social feature. They
disappear again, while the symbols and the teachings of
which they are a part, remain.

The principles of Masonry are represented in the first
three degrees, those of Entered Apprentice, Fellow Craft,
and Master Mason, and in the development of those
degrees in the Holy Royal Arch. The principles there
represented are fundamental, whether found in the York
rite, the Scottish rite, or in any other masonic rite. Some
rites have degrees which are merely local, personal, social
and inviting. There are many side rites, side issues, side
degrees, which gifted ritualists have brought into
existence, but the principles of Masonry are few and
survive the ages and their styles.

Masonry is the trunk or physical connection from
which different Orders are formed from time to time.
Rosicrucianism in the Middle Ages and other movements
of a later date were offshoots put out through members
of the Masonic Order, to meet a need of the times
without entangling Masonry itself.

In many of the forms of the masonic work that seem
trivial and childish are locked up great truths. The truths
have to be presented in some symbol or by some work,
because human beings need forms in which to see truths.
They call truths platitudes, yet cannot see them. When

truths are put into forms which are parts of physical life, an apt and striking application of such truths impresses itself upon those who see and feel the application and holds their interest.

It is possible to arrange, and Masonry does arrange, information about fundamental truths about the conscious self and its relation to nature in a systematic way, though in simple forms. By constant repetition of these forms their application to life in general becomes evident. The words used in connection with these forms become a secret language whether the forms be symbols, jewels, tools, badges, emblems, degrees, steps, signs, grips, words, ceremonies, points, lines, angles, surfaces, or simple stories. A common language is a bond of brotherhood, and a secret language which is not bestowed by birth, as is the language of one's country, but by common choice and service, is one of the strongest ties that hold men together. Also by going through these forms over and over they are engraved by sight and sound upon the breath-form and cause passive thinking along the engraved lines. Later active thinking results along the same lines, and with it comes the Light by which the particular truth concealed in the form is seen. After death the lines, made on the breath-form by masonic thinking and masonic thoughts, play an important part in shaping destiny. In the next life on earth a Mason comes under the masonic influences, though he be born under and be claimed by the spirit of a race or of a religion.

The forms of the masonic work are designed to further a discipline of feelings and desires and three minds. The desires are disciplined by thinking which sets bounds to them, and the three minds themselves are disciplined by thinking according to the forms. Only a few subjects are presented in the many masonic forms. These subjects reappear and force themselves upon the attention of a Mason. The forms after a while become suggestive of the subjects for which they stand and so engage mental activity. The discipline results from the regular exercise of the mental activity along the aspects of an inner life which the forms are designed to symbolize.

The forms preserve the secret teachings and in that respect are of inestimable value. The forms are the ancient landmarks of the Order, entrusted to the care of Masons which they are to preserve carefully and are never to suffer to be infringed.

Such are some of the purposes which the masonic play serves. Though what Masons see and hear and say and do has a deep esoteric meaning, they are not affected by that, but delight in the play, the speeches and the social features. Masons seldom, if ever, see the importance of their Order and of its purposes. When they see the inner meanings of their work and begin to live according to their teachings, they will become better men, have a broader and deeper understanding of life, and make the Order of Freemasons a living power for good in the world.

SECTION 2

Meaning of the preliminaries. A free man. Recommendation. Preparations in the heart and for initiation. The divestment. The hoodwink. The fourfold cable-tow. The candidate is the conscious self in the body. Travels. The sharp instrument. Instructions. The pledge. The three great lights and the lesser lights. What the candidate learns about these symbols. Signs, grips and words. The symbol of the lambskin. The scene of poverty. The Mason as an upright man. His working tools. Declaration of the Apprentice. The signs and their meanings. The Word. The four virtues. The six jewels. The Ground Floor of King Solomon's Temple. Purpose of the symbols and ceremonies.

BEFORE ONE can become a Freemason he must be a free man. A slave cannot be a Mason. In a wider sense he must not be a slave to lust and avarice. He must be sufficiently free to choose of his own free will and accord, that is, not be bound down by base desires or blind to the facts of life. To become a Freemason the candidate must be recommended as to character. He must be in some measure a scarcher into the mysteries of life. He must desire more light and be in search of it.

The first preparation is to be made in his heart. He appoints himself to be a Mason and prepares himself by having an honest, clean heart. When a Mason meets with such a man, he will, believing that the other will be a good member, bring the conversation on subjects which will lead the candidate to express his desire to seek admission into a lodge. After the application is made, investigated and recommended, the candidate will be prepared for admission. After he is admitted there is a further preparation for initiation in the anteroom of the lodge.

He is there divested of his clothing. That ceremony stands for the removal of the things that hold him to the outer world, such as possessions and indications of station and rank. It means that he is separated from the past, so that he can enter on a new course. When he is stripped it will appear that he is a man, not a woman. A hoodwink or blind is put over his eyes, so that he feels he is in darkness, without light, and cannot find his way. Then the thing he most desires is light.

A rope, a cable-tow — it should be a rope of four strands — is put around him. It symbolizes the bond by which all Apprentices, Craftsmen and Masons have been entered, initiated, passed and raised into the light of Masonry. The cable-tow stands for the umbilical cord by which all bodies are prepared for birth. It stands for the senses of sight, hearing, taste and smell by which the candidate (the conscious self in the body) is held after birth, which bind him to nature and lead him in darkness. It stands for Masonry which brings him out of the physical world of darkness into the Light. The cable-tow stands for the tie that binds, into a brotherhood of whatever kind. The cable-tow also is the line on the breath-form that binds one to Masonry, to destiny, to rebirth and re-existence.

He begins his work and his travels naked, in darkness, tied to humanity and its common failings. He feels the touch of a sharp instrument; his flesh is pricked to remind him of the torture to which it may put him, and that he must nevertheless persevere with the work to which he will dedicate himself. He is instructed in the conduct of life, always with his work as the end in view. He calls on God, his Triune Self, to witness his obligation and gives his pledge to preserve himself inviolate to the work. To continue his work he needs more light, and he declares that that which he most desires is light. The symbolical hoodwink or blind is removed and he is brought to light. At birth into the world the cord is severed. Likewise when the Apprentice is brought to the light, which is the new tie, the cable-tow is removed. Then he is told that the Bible, the square and the compass, on which he has taken his obligation and to which he has dedicated himself, represent the three great Lights. The three lighted candles, he is told, represent the three lesser lights: the sun, the moon and the Master of the Lodge.

If the Apprentice keeps his obligation, and does the work, he learns, by these symbols, as he advances, that he receives the Word of God, the Light of lights, through his Knower. He learns that as the compass describes a line equally distant throughout from the point around which it is drawn, so the mind, according to its light, keeps the passions and desires in bounds which are measured by reason and are of equal distance from the rightness, the center. He learns that as the square is used to draw and prove all straight lines, to make two lines at right angles to one another and to unite horizontals with perpendiculars, so by himself as the Doer all feelings and desires are made straight, are put in the right relation to each other and are united with each other.

He will learn, after he is raised, that the three great Lights are verily symbols of the three parts of his Triune Self; that the Bible, or sacred writings, which is symbolic of his Knower, which is Gnosis, is the source through which he must get Light; and that instead of the points of the compass being under the square they must be over it for him to get that Light, that is to say, Rightness, the right point, and Reason, the left point, of the compass, must set bounds to feeling, the right line, and to desire, the left line of the square.

He will learn that there are connected with him, at present, only two of the great lights, the Bible and the Compass; that the points of the square are above the compass; that is to say, his feeling and desire are not controlled by his Rightness and Reason, and that the third Light, the square, is dark, that is, the Light does not reach his feeling-and-desire. The third Light was shut out at the destruction of the first temple; it is potential only and will not be an actual Light until the temple is rebuilt.

The three lesser lights, the sun, the moon and the Master of the Lodge symbolize the body, feeling-and-desire, and their minds. The lodge is the human body. The light for the body, that is nature, is the sun. The moon reflects sunlight. The moon is feeling, on which are reflected the objects of nature by the body, which is personalized nature and is the servant of outside nature.

The third light is the Master or desire, and he ought to endeavor to rule and govern his lodge, that is, the body. The body-mind should be used to govern the body and its four senses; the feeling-mind should govern itself, and the desire-mind as the Master should govern itself in the coordination of the feelings and the control of the body.

The Apprentice, as he advances, receives the signs, grips and words, by which he can prove himself or another, in the light or in the dark, and among those not Masons, according to the degree of his light in Masonry. He learns to walk as a Mason should, on the square.

He receives a lambskin, or white apron, a symbol of his physical body. He who wears the lambskin as a badge of a Mason is thereby continually reminded of that purity of life and conduct which is necessary. The apron clothes the pelvic region and is a symbol that that should be kept clean. It refers to sex and food. As he grows in knowledge he should preserve the body not in innocence, but in purity. When he is able to wear the apron as a Master Mason should, the flap which may be an equilateral or a right-angled triangle, hangs over the square with the corners down. The apron as a square symbolizes the four elements of nature working in the fourfold body through its four systems and the four senses. The triangular flap stands for the three parts of the Triune Self, and the three minds as substitutes for the Triune Self. They are above the body or not entirely in the body in the case of the Apprentice, and within the body or fully embodied in the case of the Master.

When asked to contribute to a worthy cause the Apprentice finds he is penniless, unable to do so, naked and an object of charity. This is a reminder to aid those whom he finds in life and who are in need of help. The scene should make him feel that he is nothing more or less than what he is as a man; that he should be judged by what he is and not be valued in terms of dress, possessions, a title, or money.

He is then allowed to reclothe himself; he puts on his apron and is taken before the Master of the Lodge who directs him to stand at his right hand and tells him that he is now an upright man, a Mason, and charges him ever to walk and act as such. As a Mason, he must have working tools. He is given the working tools of an Apprentice which are the twenty-four inch gauge and common gavel.

The gauge is the symbol of masculinity. It has to do not only with the hours but with the span of life. The gauge is the rule of life and the rule of right. The first third is for the Apprentice when he should, as the masonic ritual has it, remember his Creator in the days of his youth. This is the service of God, by not wasting the creative power. Thereby he fits himself to follow his masonic work in the second degree as a Fellow Craft. He then is rebuilding his body, the temple not made with hands. The last third is for the Master Mason who is refreshed by the conserved power and is a master builder.

The gavel is said to be an instrument which operative masons use to break off the superfluous corners of rough stones to fit them for the builder's use, but with the speculative Mason the gavel stands for the force of desire which should be used with the gauge, or rule of right, to remove inherited inclinations and vices, so that each life of the Mason may be shaped into and become a living stone, a perfect ashler, in the final temple of the Triune Self. His first life, that in which he becomes an Apprentice, is said to be a corner stone, from which a super-structure of an immortal physical body is expected to rise.

The Apprentice declares that he has come into Masonry to learn to subdue his passions and improve himself in Masonry. It is the profession of his purpose. He is asked how he will know himself to be or how he may be known to be a Mason, and he declares that he will do it by certain signs, a token, a word and the perfect points of his entrance.

The signs, he says, are right angles, horizontals and perpendiculars, which must be parallel. These signs mean more than how he shall step or hold his hands or pose his body.

The right angles mean the squaring of his feeling (one line) with his desire (the other line) in all actions.

The horizontals mean the equal balancing of his feeling and of his desire.

The perpendiculars mean that his feeling and desire are raised to uprightness from lowness.

The token is a grip. It means that he must hold his feeling and his desire with a firm grip, and it also means that feeling and desire should grip each other in the same degree and prove each other.

A word is the one used in the Apprentice degree, and is a symbol. Lines make letters, and letters a word. Four letters are needed to make The Word. The Apprentice can supply only one letter, that letter is A and is made of two lines, feeling and desire. The Word is found by the Royal Arch Mason.

The perfect points of the Apprentice's entrance are four. They are the four cardinal virtues: temperance is habitual self-restraint or control of one's passionate impulses and appetites; fortitude means constant courage, patience and endurance without fear of danger; prudence means skill in right thinking and in the performance of right action; and justice is knowledge of the rights of oneself and others, and in thinking and acting in accordance with that knowledge.

The candidate learns about the jewels. There are six jewels, three movable, which are the rough ashler, the perfect ashler, and the trestle-board. The rough ashler is the symbol of the present, imperfect physical body; the perfect ashler is the symbol of the physical body after it has been perfected, and the trestle-board the symbol of the breath-form, on which the designs of the building are drawn. These three jewels are called movable because they perish after each life or are carried from life to life. The immovable jewels are the square, the level and the plumb. The square symbolizes desire, the level feeling and the plumb the pattern of the perfect body which is on the breath-form. These three are called immovable, because they are of the Triune Self and do not die.

The First Degree, that of Entered Apprentice, relates to the initiation of himself as Doer of feeling-and-desire. This is done on the Ground Floor of Solomon's Temple, that is, in the pelvic region. The Apprentice first prepares himself in his heart, then he is prepared for initiation by being separated from his past. After he has traveled, has been brought to light, has received some information about the three greater Lights by means of the three lesser lights, has received his white apron, is clothed again and has seen the blazing star, he is given the working tools of an Entered Apprentice and then makes certain declarations. All of the symbols and ceremonies are intended to impress upon him what to do with his desires and the use of his desire-mind, feeling-mind, and body-mind in his conduct towards himself, his brothers, and his God.

SECTION 3

The degree of Fellow Craft. How the candidate is received and the meaning of it. Being brought to light. What he receives. The tools of a Fellow Craft. Their meaning. The two Columns. Building the bridge from Boaz to Jachin. The three, five and seven steps. The Middle Chamber. Meaning of the steps. The wages and the jewels. Meaning of the letter G. The point and the circle. The four and the three degrees. The twelve points on the circle. The Zodiacal signs. Expression of universal truths. Geometry. The achievements of the Fellow Craft. The Thinker. The Master Mason. Preparation. Reception. Being brought to light. The pass, the grip, the apron and the tools of a Master Mason.

T HE SECOND DEGREE, that of Fellow Craft, is not an initiation of the Thinker, but is the passing of the conscious Doer from the darkness and ignorance of feeling-and-desire to the light of Rightness-and-Reason. He is received into this degree on the angle of the square, symbolic of the fact that he has made his feeling-and-desire right and square, at right angles with each other, that he has united them, and that they will be used so in all his actions. He asks for more light and is shown how to step towards that Light. He receives more Light. In being brought to Light in this degree, he perceives one point of the compass above the square, symbolic of the fact that he receives Light through the Rightness of his Thinker and that he will be guided in his actions from that point, that Light. He receives the pass, the grip and the word of a Fellow Craft. The pass is symbolical of the transfer or passage from the first to the second degree. The grip stands for the power of Rightness over feeling-and-desire. The word is still not the Word, but is only two letters, namely the A with a U or an O.

He is given the working tools of a Fellow Craft which are the plumb, the square and the level. The plumb stands for uprightness in thinking, the level for equality in thinking, and the square for the union of the plumb and the level. This means that the signs which were only lines in the Apprentice degree have now in the Fellow Craft degree become tools; the perpendiculars and horizontals, which were lines, have become the plumb and the level, and the right angles have become the square. Desire and feeling are now upright and level, united, that is, in agreement with and in right relation to each other, and act from the point of their union which is at Rightness. The angle of the square stands for the point of union. The square is used in thinking, whether by the plumb or on the level, in all that concerns the earth, that is, the physical body of oneself or of another.

He is shown two brazen columns, said to have been at the entrance of Solomon's Temple. Boaz, the left column, symbolizes the sympathetic or nature column, which will be in front of the body, and Jachin, the right one, is the spinal column, the column of the Triune Self. When the

Doer part of the Triune Self first came into its body, that is, its temple, the body was neither male nor female, and the two columns existed and functioned having the united power. After its temple was destroyed, the Doer functioned in a body which was either male or female and had only Jachin, the male column, and had only the power of the male or of the female. Boaz does not exist, except potentially. The Fellow Craft is reminded by seeing the two columns that he has to rebuild Boaz. The stones which the Apprentice has prepared with his rule and gavel are to be further prepared by the Fellow Craft for the Master Mason before Boaz will be re-established. It is significant that the chapiters of both columns show network, lily-work and pomegranates full of seeds. The network is that of interlaced nerves which is built up by purity which preserves the seeds, and which builds the bridge from Boaz to Jachin.

The Fellow Craft sees the three, five and seven steps or stairs as the winding stairs leading to the Middle Chamber of Solomon's Temple. The five steps are symbolic of work in the Fellow Craft degree, while the three steps relate to the Apprentice degree through which he has passed and the work of which he continues.

The three, five and seven steps or stairs are certain centers or organs in the body. The body as a whole is King Solomon's Temple (or the ruins of it from which the temple is to be rebuilt). The entrance or first step is the prostate, the second step symbolizes the kidneys, the third the adrenals, the fourth the heart, the fifth the lungs, the sixth the pituitary body and the seventh the pineal body. These steps are taken by the use of the minds of Rightness and of Reason. The body-mind is used by the Apprentice to control the body, the feeling-mind to control feeling and the desire-mind to control desire. By controlling feeling he controls feelings, and by controlling desire, he controls desires. The candidate is always the Doer part of the Triune Self, throughout the work of the three degrees. His taking the five steps of the Fellow Craft means the ability to reach the minds used by and for Rightness and Reason of the Thinker of his Triune Self. His taking the seven steps symbolizes his reaching to the minds which are used by and for I-ness and selfness.

The white apron or clean body, which is the badge of a Mason, the rule of right and the gavel of desire are the three steps; by them the Apprentice prepares stones for building. The five are the same three together with the two, the plumb and the level, added. When uprightness in thinking is united with equality in thinking, the plumb and the level form the square, the point of union being at rightness. With these five the Fellow Craft prepares and fits the building stones. The building stones are the units of nature. The seven are a symbol for the seven minds and seven powers of the minds to develop which the Fellow Craft is called. Speculative Masonry designates these seven aspects by the names of the liberal arts and sciences, which are given as grammar, rhetoric, logic, arithmetic, geometry, music and astronomy. The great Three, Five and Seven, though here mentioned, are not brought into the ritual, except that the three, five and seven are brought into relation with the development of the Doer of feeling-and-desire to use its minds.

The ascent through a porch, by a flight of winding stairs, consisting of three, five and seven steps, to a place representing the Middle Chamber of King Solomon's Temple, that is, the lodge working in the Fellow Craft degree, is also symbolical of various windings of nature to her concealed recesses, that is, certain physiological developments, due to the development of one's minds, by thinking, before he is received and recorded as a Fellow Craft.

The wages and jewels he receives for his work as a Fellow Craft are certain psychic and mental powers, symbolized by corn, wine and oil, and by the attentive ear, instructive tongue and faithful breast.

The attention of the Fellow Craft is directed to a great symbol placed above the head of the Master, the letter G. It is said to stand for God, for Gnosis and for Geometry. But it has not been at all times a Roman G. The G stands in place of that which is universally symbolized by the point in the center of a circle.

The point and the circle are the same, the point is the infinitesimally small circle and the circle is the point fully expressed. The expression is divided into the manifested and the unmanifested. The expression proceeds by points and lines. The unmanifested is present in the manifested and the manifested is in the unmanifested. The purpose of the expression is to make that which becomes manifested, conscious of and to identify itself with the unmanifested which is within it; then the circle is fully expressed and the expression, by degrees, re-becomes the point. The expression is divided into the unmanifested or Substance and the manifested or matter. Matter is again

divided into nature-matter and intelligent-matter, according to degrees in which the matter is conscious. These
degrees are proved by the square and described by the
compass, according to angles, horizontals and perpendiculars. Nature-matter is divided infinitely according to
the subdegrees of the four elements, and their combina-
tions and subdivisions, and their hierarchies of beings in
the four manifested worlds. Intelligent-matter, that is,
the Triune Self, is divided into three degrees, those of
Apprentice, Fellow Craft and Master. These are exalted
in the Royal Arch, which is in Substance, beyond matter.
The unmanifested is always in the manifested on the
nature-side as well as on the intelligent-side, but it can be
approached and found in the intelligent-side only. It is
found by being conscious, which in Masonry is called getting more Light.

The point and the circle stand for all this and for more.
The meaning of the fully expressed circle can be rendered
by symbols, twelve in number, which stand for twelve
points on the circle. Every being and thing in the
manifested worlds and the unmanifested universe has a
sharply marked value, nature and place, according to
some of these points.

The best symbols to indicate the twelve points of the
circle are the Zodiacal signs. Universal truths can be expressed through the Zodiac in a way which ordinary
language does not permit and so can be understood, after
a fashion, by men. To illustrate, the Universe, as well as a
cell, is divided by a line from Cancer to Capricorn into
the unmanifested above and the manifested below. Matter is separated by a line from Aries to Libra into

nature-matter and intelligent-matter. "Souls" enter by conception at the gate of Cancer of the physical world, and are born at the gate of Libra and pass on at the gate of Capricorn. The square is made by the line from Cancer to Libra and by the line from Libra to Capricorn, and the Master sits in the East, at Capricorn, and rules his lodge on this square, the angle of which is at Libra. The square of the Great Architect is the square from Cancer to Libra to Capricorn of the Universe, over and above the four worlds of Cancer, Leo, Virgo, and Libra. So the signs of the Zodiac, as symbols of the twelve points of the fully expressed circle, speak an accurate language that reaches everything in the Universe. This language is that for which the word Geometry stands. The Fellow Craft, is told that this is also symbolized by the letter G.

Geometry is half of the science, the other half is the geometer. Geometry deals with only one of the tools, namely the square, which is used to draw straight lines, horizontals and perpendiculars, and to prove corners. The other tool, the compass, stands for the other half, the Geometer, or the Intelligence, without which there could be no Geometry. The compass draws curved lines between two points and describes a circle which is one continuous line without end, each part of which is equally distant from the center. Within the bounds of the circle, all true building must be erected on the square.

The Apprentice has passed into the Fellow Craft. The Fellow Craft has received more Light and has learned the use of his tools; he understands how to rebuild the two columns and how to ascend the winding stairs by the three, five and seven steps. The symbols and the work in this degree relate to the minds of feeling-and-desire coming under the guidance of the minds of Rightness and Reason of the Thinker of the Triune Self. By the plumb and the level of his thinking the Fellow Craft adjusts feeling-and-desire. He causes all the feelings and desires to be squared on the inner as well as on the outer expressions. He does all this by his thinking.

The degree of Master Mason represents the Apprentice and Fellow Craft raised to the degree of Master. As the Apprentice is the Doer and the Fellow Craft the Thinker, so the Master Mason is the Knower. Going through each degree as an individual symbolizes the development of the Apprentice or Doer passing to the Fellow Craft or relation to the Thinker and being raised to the degree of Master Mason or attaining to relation to the Knower.

The candidate after he is prepared, blindfolded and tied with cable-tow around his waist, enters the lodge. He is received on both points of the compass, pressed against his breast. He takes the three steps to the altar where he kneels for the third time, rests his hands on the Bible, square and compass, and takes the obligation of a Master Mason. He asks for further light in Masonry. He is brought to light by the Master of the lodge, and hoodwink and cable-tow removed. Thus he sees that both points of the compass are above the square. This is a symbol that with one who has reached this degree both aspects of the Thinker are operative above feeling-and-desire because feeling-and-desire have put themselves under the guidance of the Thinker. He receives the pass and grip of a Master Mason and wears his apron as a Master Mason, that is, with the flap and all corners down.

The working tools of a Master are all the implements of Masonry of the three degrees, more especially the trowel. As the gauge and mallet prepared the rough stones, as the plumb, level and square fitted them into position, so the trowel spreads the cement and completes the work of the Apprentice and Fellow Craft.

SECTION 4

Life, death and resurrection of Hiram Abiff. The great lesson of Masonry. What Hiram symbolizes. The two triangles. The designs on the trestle-board. The South gate. The workmen. Hiram is restrained from going out. He is slain at the East gate. The immortal body. Jubela, Jubelo, Jubelum. Meanings of these three symbols. The three assaults. The Masonic drama. The fifteen workmen. The Great Twelve. The pairs of triangles forming six-pointed stars. Hiram as the power that makes the round. The finding of the three ruffians. The three burials of Hiram. The raising by King Solomon. The monument at the place of burial. Raising of the candidate. The three columns. The forty-seventh problem of Euclid.

T HE REMAINING portion of the initiation is a masonic drama, representing the life, death and resurrection of Hiram Abiff, whose part the candidate is made to take. Hiram was the master builder of King Solomon's Temple and was slain by workmen for his refusal to impart the Word to them, and after two burials was raised by King Solomon and then buried the third time. This story conceals the great lesson of Masonry.

Hiram is the seminal principle, the generative power, the sex power, not an organ, not the fluid, but the power, invisible and most mysterious. This power lies in the

Conscious Light of the Intelligence which is carried by
desire and is an extract from the four elements, prepared
by the four systems of the body. This power, having
therefore something of the seven faculties of the
Intelligence, something of the three parts of the Triune
Self, and something of the four elements, is to be found
only in a human body. This power is concentrated
monthly by the inner brain, so becomes the lunar germ,
and as such descends along the sympathetic nervous
system in the front of the body and gathers Light of the
Intelligence as it proceeds. The lunar germ in man is a
concentration of the whole power, but one half of the
power is checked in its possible development. A man,
symbolized according to the language for which the
masonic word Geometry stands, by the triangle Cancer,
Scorpio and Pisces, has only half the power, and so has a
woman, symbolized by the female triangle Taurus, Virgo
and Capricorn. The other half in each is dormant or
suppressed. The active half develops in the body organs
to express itself and is lost through them. With this loss
are mingled thoughts of lust, violence, shame, dishonor,
disease, love and hate, which are the cable-tow of rebirth.
If Hiram is not lost, but is saved, the half of him that is
checked will develop in the body and there will build new
parts, new organs, new channels. Hiram is the builder.

Hiram, the Master-Builder, the Grand Master, draws
his designs on the trestle-board — that is, the lines on the
breath-form which is in the sympathetic nervous system
— and passes out each day, that is, each life, through the
South gate, Libra, of the outer courts of the Temple.
That is to say, the monthly germ is lost. It is his usual

custom to enter the unfinished Sanctum Sanctorum, that is, the heart and lungs, on the line Cancer to Capricorn. There thinking draws out the lines of his designs upon the trestle-board, whereby the craft pursue their labors, that is, whereby the workmen or elementals in the four systems of the body build according to the lines, the physical state and circumstances in which the body exists.

On one day, that is, in one life, when Hiram, following his usual custom attempts to leave the body at the South gate, the gate of sex, he is hindered and restrained from going out. He turns, seeks to go out at the West gate, Cancer, and is again prevented. Then he seeks the East gate, Capricorn, and there he is slain. This means that the sex power sought to leave by the sex opening and when that was barred, by the opening in the breasts, that is, by emotions, and when that was closed, by a place in the spine, which stands for the brain or intellect, and when that exit, too, was blocked, it died to these mortal expressions of itself. Having so died to mortality and corruption it was raised to build an incorruptible and immortal body.

The three ruffians Jubela, Jubelo and Jubelum, are no ruffians, but are the Junior Warden, Senior Warden and Worshipful Master, the three officers of the lodge, in Masonry, and they stand also for the three parts of the Triune Self, Jubela being the Doer, Jubelo the Thinker, and Jubelum the Knower. Each has a part of the Word. If their parts were combined they would be AUM or AOM or three of the four parts of the Word. But no combination is made, that is, the three parts do not work coordinately.

Hiram has the Word, he is the Word, for he has the Light, that is, the Intelligence powers and the Triune Self powers and the powers of the four elements, and he has them combined. When assaulted by the first ruffian and asked for the Word, Hiram, therefore, says: "Wait until the Temple is completed," that is, until he has built the immortal body. He says about giving the secrets of the Word: "I cannot; nor can they be given, except in the presence of Solomon, King of Israel (the Knower), and Hiram, King of Tyre (the Thinker), and myself" The Doer (the Light in the sex with feeling-and-desire). This means that the Word cannot be imparted by the sex power since the sex power only builds the immortal body, the Temple. When Hiram as the combined powers of the Light, the Doer and the sexes, has completed the building of the body he can act his own part as Hiram, the Doer of feeling-and-desire. Then together with the Thinker, King of Tyre, and the Knower, Solomon, he is the Word and enters the finished Temple.

Hiram is many things. He is the mysterious creative power hidden in the powers of the sexes, hence he is the builder, the Master Builder, he is the Lost Word, being the Doer which is lost, because it is immersed in flesh and blood and does not know itself in the human being; and he is the combined powers of the Light and of the Triune Self and of the nature powers of the sexes when he has found himself in the ruins of the temple and is conscious of himself as the Triune Self.

Jubela, Jubelo and Jubelum are ruffians in so far as they are not performing the true functions of their offices. They are said to be ruffians because they act as the Doer part in its Thinker and Knower aspects, when it is the false "I." The three are only the Doer part in the three aspects of its Triune Self. Jubela gives Hiram a blow with the gauge, a tool of the Apprentice, across the throat, according to the ritual. This is a blind for the sex part. Jubelo strikes Hiram with the square, a tool of the Fellow Craft, across the breast, and Jubelum fells him with a setting-maul, the gavel of a Master. The gauge is the line, the square the surface, and the maul the cube.

Hiram has so far gone out of the South gate, his custom in the bodies of the run of human beings. The masonic drama refers to a time when it is discovered that the sex power holds the key to all secrets and to all power. To wrest the key from this power the human being restrains it from going out. Mere restraint does not obtain the secret, but the power, when controlled, rises, passing from the sex functions into the four physical bodies. Then the human being prevents Hiram from leaving by thoughts, at the emotional center. But Hiram does not yield the secret, because the human being practices the restraint from selfish motives to get power, and not to rebuild the Temple, and because the human being is physically and psychically incapable of holding the power. Hiram passes to the East and there meets Jubelum who, though in the true aspect he is the Knower, is in the drama the false "I," an egotistical aspect of the Doer. To him Hiram cannot impart the Word. Yet, the human being, though from selfish motives, has so far advanced that there is no more physical reproduction. This is symbolized by the slaying of Hiram.

In the conspiracy to obtain the secret of Hiram were fifteen workmen. Twelve recanted and the remaining three, Jubela, Jubelo and Jubelum, carried out the plot. The twelve here are the twelve points on the Zodiac in the body, the three are the double aspects of the Doer, and the body-mind. The twelve represent numbers, that is, twelve ultimate beings and orders of beings.

Everything in the manifested Universe is in some measure representative of the Great Twelve. The human body is their organ. The more a human being develops, the more will he have in him live centers representing and responding to the Great Twelve. King Solomon sends the twelve workmen in the body in search of the ruffians. He sends three East, three North, three South, and three West. He sends Taurus, Virgo and Capricorn to act in the East, Leo, Sagittary and Aries in the North, Aquarius, Gemini and Libra in the South, and Scorpio, Pisces and Cancer in the West. Of these triads, those of Leo, Aries, and Sagittary, and of Gemini, Libra and Aquarius are universal, the first triangle operating through the second. The triad of Taurus, Virgo and Capricorn operates through that of Cancer, Scorpio and Pisces, and both are human. Each pair of triads forms a six-pointed star. There is the universal hexad, the macrocosm, and the human hexad, the microcosm. The universal hexad, composed of the sexless triad, Aries, Leo, Sagittary and the androgynous triad, Gemini, Libra and Aquarius, is God or Supreme Intelligence, and nature. The human hexad is composed of the Cancer, Scorpio and Pisces triad, pointing West, which is man or the male triad, and of Taurus, Virgo and Capricorn, pointing East, which is woman, the female triad.

The macrocosmic and the microcosmic signs are represented in the human body by twelve parts and centers, each having its special character. The human body therefore is potentially a complete universe. The six universal signs are centers at which the six human signs can act if the human signs come together in any one of those six. For instance, if the male and female triads unite at their points of Scorpio and Virgo in Libra, they procreate through the universal gate of sex of the nature triad. But if the male and female triads at their points of Scorpio and Capricorn unite at Sagittary, the sexless gate of the universal triad, they create a thought. Though the twelve powers are represented in a human body, they cannot act freely and fully, but are restrained, paralyzed, half dead, impotent, except the powers represented by Virgo, Scorpio, and Libra, that is, the female in a female body, the male in a male body, and the sex in both bodies.

Hiram is the power that makes the rounds of the twelve centers, that strengthens and empowers them, builds up the twelve centers, makes them alive and fits them so that they can be related to the Great Twelve, and so that the Doer in the body can act with the Great Twelve.

King Solomon's sending the twelve workmen in search of the three ruffians means that after Hiram is slain, within the meaning of the legend, the Knower part which is in contact with the body commands the twelve powers in the body to locate the three ruffians who have brought about the death of Hiram, who are the false "I" in its three aspects. The three ruffians are found near the body of the slain, that is, the physical suppression of the sex power, and are executed. They are condemned for having tried to get the power from Hiram before they were qualified to receive it.

Hiram was buried three times. First the ruffians buried him in the rubbish of the Temple, that is, the sex power was turned into the foods of the body to build it up. At night they came back to give the body a more decent burial. They carried it West, to the brow of the hill West of Mount Moriah, that is, the sex power was buried in or turned into psychic power. There it was discovered by a party of workmen. After it had been raised by King Solomon himself by the strong grip or lion's paw — which is the grip identified with a life like that of Jesus, the lion of the Tribe of Judah so-called from the alleged heraldic lion of the Tribe — it was buried near the Sanctum Sanctorum of King Solomon's Temple, that is, the sex power was turned into the spine.

The raising by Solomon is significant. The body could not be raised by the grip of the Entered Apprentice, nor by that of the Fellow Craft, that is the Doer could not, either with the psychic or its mental aspect raise or transmute the mortal into an immortal body. It required the Knower, here King Solomon himself, to raise Hiram. King Solomon had the assistance of Hiram, King of Tyre, the Thinker, and of the brethren, that is, the powers in the body.

The tradition of Masonry is that a monument was erected to the memory of Hiram, at his place of burial. The monument represents a virgin weeping over a broken column. Before her was an open book, behind her stood

Time. It is a reminder of the destruction of the original temple, at which the Boaz column, which represented the female column in the temple of man was broken. The vestige or monument is the sternum, which is all that is left. The virgin is the woman weeping over her own broken column. Time is death, as the continuous passing of the events; and the open book is the breath-form and aia, which bear the record of what happened. The female figure is also the widow, as the broken column, who was the mother of Hiram, weeping for the male power, which she lost when the column was broken. Hiram is the son of a widow; he is unprotected and has had to wander along the labyrinth of the alimentary canal since the column was broken.

The destruction of the temple occurs in every life. Hiram is not allowed to rebuild it. In this sense he is slain in every life. At each life he is resurrected and tries to rebuild the temple beginning with the re-establishment of the column, which is broken. The Monument of the woman with her broken column is a reminder that a Mason must re-establish the broken column in himself as the requisite to rebuild his temple, and he can re-establish the column only by keeping Hiram in the body to rebuild it. Hiram has within him the original plan of the immortal body which, when rebuilt, will be greater than the first temple.

The candidate having been made to take the part of Hiram is finally raised by King Solomon, the Master of the Lodge, by the real grip of a Master Mason, and on the five points of fellowship, or five points of the body. The brethren assist in raising the candidate to a standing position. The hoodwink is slipped off his eyes. After he has received an historical account of the events he passed through as Hiram, the Master explains the various symbols. He uses them as subjects for moral exhortations and rules.

The three grand masonic columns or pillars, designated Wisdom, Strength, and Beauty, stand for the three parts of the body. They also stand for parts of the Triune Self. In this connection the pillar of Wisdom is Solomon, the spinal or Jachin column; the pillar of Strength is Hiram, King of Tyre, the sympathetic or Boaz column; and the pillar of Beauty is Hiram Abiff, the bridge or bridge builder, between the two.

The forty-seventh problem of Euclid is more than a moral exhortation. It means that when the male (desire) and the female (feeling) in one physical body work together they build a new body equal to their sum. The new body, the square of the hypotenuse, is the temple rebuilt.

After the candidate has been raised to the degree of Master Mason, he represents the Doer, Thinker, and Knower, each developed to its capacity and co-ordinated so that they are a trinity, the Triune Self. This trinity is in Masonry represented as a right-angled triangle in the lodge.

SECTION 5

Meaning of the lodge as a room and as the brothers. The officers, their stations and duties. The three degrees as the foundation of Masonry. The work. A Mason's own lodge.

THE LODGE as a room or hall is an oblong square, which is a half of a perfect square, and which is inside or outside the lower half of a circle. Each lodge meets in the same room, alike furnished, but the lodge working in the Apprentice degree is styled the Ground Floor, the lodge working the Fellow Craft degree is called the Middle Chamber, and the lodge working the Master degree is called the Sanctum Sanctorum, all in King Solomon's Temple. The lodge in this sense symbolizes, with the present day humanity, the part of the body from the breasts and from the back opposite the breasts to the sex. When the temple is rebuilt the Ground Floor will be the pelvic section, the Middle Chamber the abdominal section, and the Sanctum Sanctorum the thoracic section.

The lodge, as a number of brothers who compose it, represents certain working centers and their activities in the body of a Mason. These are shown by the officers stationed in the West, South and East. These are the three without whom there can be no lodge. The breasts, standing for the Boaz column, where the sternum is, are the station of the Senior Warden in the West. The places of the coccygeal gland and anus, which are the ends of the two tubes, are the station of the Junior Warden in the South. A place in the spinal cord opposite the heart is the station of the Master in the East.

The Senior Deacon in front of and to the right of the Master, and the Junior Deacon at the right and in front of the Senior Warden make five, and the Secretary at the left and the Treasurer at the right of the Master, make seven. These are the seven officers of the lodge. In addition there are the two stewards, one on each side of the Junior Warden in the South, and the Tyler, the guard at the door.

The Senior Warden's duty is to strengthen and support the Master and assist him in carrying on the work of the lodge.

The Junior Warden's duty, according to the ritual, is to observe and record the time, to call the craft from labor to refreshment, to superintend that, to keep them from intemperance or excess and to call them to labor again. His station is there but there is no organ or conduit from Boaz to Jachin. His duty is to observe the time, that is, sun time, the Master standing for the sun, and moon time, the Senior Warden for the moon. This relates to sex power, the moon, and to Doer power, the sun, that is to say, the duty of that center is to observe the time and the seasons of the lunar and solar germs. He should call the craft, that is, the Masons working in the part of the temple called the lodge, and the elemental workmen who labor outside, in the quarries, in other parts of the body. The four senses and the elementals in the systems all go to the sex center to get refreshment. The center of the Junior Warden should balance the forces of Boaz and Jachin and with these forces refresh the workmen of the temple.

"As the sun rises in the East to open and govern the day, so rises the Master in the East to open and govern his lodge, set the craft to work and give them proper instructions," says the ritual. The Master is the sun, represented by the solar germ, in the body, as the Senior Warden is the moon. The Master dispenses his light from his seat in the East, that is, the spinal cord back of the heart, to the Senior Warden at the breasts, through whom his orders are issued.

The remaining officers of the lodge, considered as centers in the body, are assistants to these three main officers, near whom they are stationed and whose orders they execute. The Secretary and Treasurer record and keep on the breath-form the accounts of the transactions of the lodge, which are carried over from lodge to lodge, that is from life to life.

The lodge as a number of brothers who compose it stands also for the embodied Doer portions or contacts of the Triune Self and their aspects. The Junior Warden is the Doer and his two stewards are the active and the passive side of desire-and-feeling. The Senior Warden represents the Thinker and the Junior Deacon is the active side, called reason. The Master is the Knower and the Senior Deacon is I-ness, the passive aspect. It may be noted that the Senior Warden and the Master have each only one assistant.

The degrees of Entered Apprentice, Fellow Craft and
Master Mason, are the foundations of Masonry, which is
the building of an immortal body. The Entered
Apprentice is the Doer, the Fellow Craft the Thinker,
and the Master Mason the Knower in contact with the
body. They carry on the work of the lodge in the trunk of
the body and are assisted by the other officers. The work
of the lodge is kept before the eyes of Masons by the
opening of the lodge, the order of business, the initiating,
passing and raising of candidates and the closing of the
lodge. All is done with impressiveness and becoming
dignity. The real work is the initiating, passing and
raising of the Doer-in-the-body to conscious relation with
its Thinker and Knower parts.

Every Mason should open his own lodge, that is, begin
in the morning the work of the day with the dignity of the
opening of his masonic lodge. He should recognize the
stations and duties of the parts and their centers in the
body and charge them to see that the workmen, that is,
the elementals functioning in the body, are properly
employed. He should recognize that he is the candidate
to be initiated by the trials of the day, and that he must
pass through them with temperance, fortitude, prudence
and justice, so that he may be exalted and receive more
Light.

SECTION 6

The cable-tow. The Royal Arch. The candidate as the keystone. Realization of the great Masonic symbol. The fifth degree. The fourth degree. The keystone with the mark of Hiram. The sixth degree. Another aspect of the keystone symbol. The union of Boaz and Jachin. The Glory of the Lord fills the Lord's house. The seventh degree. The Tabernacle. The Master's jewels and the Ark of the Covenant. The Name and the Word.

T HE CABLE-TOW of the four senses leads the candidate (the Doer-in-the-body) through each of the four great degrees of Masonry, until the senses cease to be ties. The Master Mason receives More Light in the Chapter or Holy Royal Arch, which is in the North. This is the Fourth Degree. The Lodge is an oblong square in the lower half of the circle; the Chapter is another oblong square, which together with the first, forms a perfect square, within the circle, and that part of the circle which is the arc above or North of this square, is the Royal Arch. Into that, when the cable-tow no longer leads him the candidate is fitted as a keystone. This Fourth Degree has, however, in the course of time been stretched out and cut into four degrees, of which the Fourth, Sixth, and Seventh Degrees contain the work of the original Fourth Degree.

The Royal Arch is the culmination and consummation of the three degrees of Entered Apprentice, Fellow Craft and Master Mason. The great Masonic symbol of compass and square is there realized. The three points of the square are those three lower degrees, and the compass, so joined with them as to make a six-pointed star, now, in the Royal Arch Degrees, represent the Light of the Intelligence, which in the Conscious Light of the Royal Arch Mason is the threefold Light that has come into his noetic, his mental and his psychic atmospheres. This state of a Mason is the subject of which various aspects are symbolized by the work of the Fourth, Sixth and Seventh Degrees, relating to the Light of the Intelligence when the Glory of the Lord fills the House, to the keystone when the arch is completed, to the Word when it is found, and to the Name when the divided Adam or Jehovah becomes one.

In the Fifth Degree, that of Past Master, the candidate takes the obligation of a Master of the Lodge, and upon being installed is made to see and feel his inability to keep the turbulent brethren sufficiently in order to conduct the work of the Lodge. This degree is a mere filler for ceremonial purposes.

The Fourth Degree or that of Mark Master is said to have been instituted by King Solomon for the purpose of detecting impostors. Each workman was required to put his distinctive mark upon the product of his labor. The Mark Master could thereby detect impostors and could notice unfinished and imperfect work. This degree is dedicated to Hiram, the builder, and its characteristic is the keystone he had fashioned and on which was his mark. This stone possessing merits unknown to the builders was rejected by them but became the "chief stone of the corner."

In the lodge in which the Master Mason is to be advanced to the Fourth, or honorary, Degree of Mark Master, the brethren, during the opening, gather round a miniature of King Solomon's Temple, — symbol of the temple into which they are to rebuild their bodies — which is erected on the middle of the floor. During the opening the Master says to them: "Ye also, as living stones, be ye built up a spiritual house, an holy priesthood, to offer up sacrifices acceptable to God."

The candidate being duly and truly prepared and carrying a keystone is conducted into the lodge. Two of the brethren who carry oblong stones, and the candidate with his keystone, present the stones as specimens of their work. The two stones carried by the companions are received for the temple, but the keystone, being neither oblong nor square, is rejected as of no account and is heaved over among the rubbish of the temple where Hiram was buried at one time. For want of a keystone to one of the principal arches the workmen are disturbed. The Right Worshipful Master, representing King Solomon, says that he gave Hiram Abiff, the Grand Master, orders to make that keystone, previous to his assassination, and inquires if such a stone has not been brought up for inspection. The keystone which the candidate had brought and had seen heaved over into the rubbish, is found and is now received and becomes the "head of the corner."

The keystone has on it the mark of Hiram. The

keystone is Hiram transformed into a certain lunar germ, which was preserved, died to the world, rose along the spine, and ascended into the head. Hiram's mark is a double cross made by a stationary cross H.S.W.K. and a movable cross T.T.S.S. The import of these crosses can be known by the meaning of the Zodiacal signs which these eight points of the crosses represent on the circumference of the circle. His mark is his new name, a name of an Order of beings to which he now belongs. This new name is written on a white stone, or the purified essence, that is the vesture of Hiram. Hiram, having overcome, has eaten of the hidden manna, that is, has received the Light accumulated by successive lunar germs. The keystone that has the mark of Hiram, also stands for the candidate himself who has overcome, who has ascended into the hill of the Lord and who shall stand in his holy place.

The Sixth Degree, that of the Most Excellent Master, is the initiation of the candidate by the descent of the Light into the completed temple, or, in Masonic language, when the Glory of the Lord fills the House. In his obligation the candidate promises that he will dispense light and knowledge to all ignorant and uninformed brethren.

Another aspect of the keystone is emphasized by the ceremonies which take up again the teaching of the stone with Hiram's mark, that is, the candidate himself. The ceremonies now represent the day for the celebration of the capstone, copestone, or keystone. The keystone is made to close an arch placed on the two columns Boaz and Jachin. This is a symbol that the physical body has been rebuilt, that an arch over Boaz and Jachin unites them above and another arch unites them below. This is done as the result of the action of the Junior Warden in the first three degrees. He harmonized the male and female forces in the West and East columns, at the South, Libra, and with these equilibrated forces built the arches, or bridges, below and above. With the arch above and the keystone inserted therein, the temple is completed.

The Light of the Intelligence descends into the candidate and fills his body. The Glory of the Lord fills the Lord's House. The mortal body has been transformed into an immortal body. This culmination of the Masonic purpose is sometimes represented by the fire coming down from heaven and by a temple in the lodge being filled with effulgent light. Sometimes a passage from the Bible is read and an illumination made to show to the candidate the lodge filled with the glory that floods the temple.

In the Seventh Degree or Royal Arch are symbolized events which preceded the completion of the temple, and some information is given about the Word.

The candidate is made to represent one of three Masons who after the destruction of Jerusalem by Nebuchadnezzar were captives in Babylon till Cyrus of Persia liberated them. They returned to Jerusalem to assist in building the temple. On arrival they found the Tabernacle, a temporary structure. This is the temporary physical body, which serves until the temple is rebuilt. The three were given tools and directed to begin their labors at the North East corner of the ruined temple.

There they discovered a secret vault under a trap which was the keystone of an arch. The keystone taken before the Grand Council was there discovered to be the keystone of the principal arch in Solomon's Temple. Lowered by cable-tow into the vault the candidate finds three small trying-squares which are by the Grand Council recognized as the Master's Jewels of King Solomon, of King Hiram of Tyre and of Hiram Abiff. On another descent a small box is found which is recognized by the Grand Council as the Ark of the Covenant. Out of this chest are taken a pot of manna and four pieces of paper containing in right angles and dots the key to a mystery language. With this key three mysterious words written in triangular form upon the Ark, become readable as the name of God in the Chaldaic, Hebrew and Syriac languages; and this Name of the Deity is in the ritual said to be the long lost Master Mason's Word or Logos. This identification among modern Masons of the Name and the Word is a blind, or is due to a mistake.

The Name and the Word are distinct and not the same. The Name is a name, one of the names, of the God of the physical world, the Earth Spirit. This God belongs to the nature-side. It is known by different names in different ages among different peoples. Brahma is one of the names; originally it was Brahm and after it divided it became Brahma, and then the Trimurti Brahma-Vishnu-Shiva. This is the Name of the God of the physical world, with the Hindus. The name of the Triune Self, however, is BrahmA, VishnU, BrahM, the last letters of which are the Word.

The Hebrew Name is Jehovah, and modern Masons

have adopted this. It is a name of the ruler of the physical world and its four planes. This God has no physical body except the formless four elements in the physical world and the human bodies of those who are born in his Name and who obey his laws. At one time this God acted through human physical bodies which were sexless, then he acted through human bodies which were bi-sexual, and now he acts through human bodies that are male human bodies and that are female human bodies. The Name can be pronounced only when a human body has in it active masculine and passive feminine powers. A man can only give half of the Name, because his body is only half the Name. To this fact refers the Masonic practice of saying: "I will letter it or halve it." The Name is the name of the body and the body must be rebuilt into a balanced male-female body before it is the Name and the dweller in the body can breathe the Name. The Name belongs to the body, is of the four elements and hence has four letters, Jod, He, Vav, He. The Name is ineffable until such time as it can be breathed by the dweller in a normal balanced or sexless physical body.

The Word, an English translation of the Logos, as used by St. John, is not the Name. It is an expression of the full Triune Self powers, each of the three parts being represented in it by a sound, and the perfect body in which the Triune Self dwells being also represented by a sound. The Doer part is expressed as A, the Thinker part as U or O, the Knower part as M, and the perfect body as I. The Word is I-A-O-M, in four sylables or letters. The expression of the perfect body and the Triune Self as these sounds is an expression of the Conscious Light of the Intelligence through that Self and body. When a part in its physical body sounds as IAOM each of the parts sounds AOM, and each represents a Logos. The Knower is then the First Logos, the Thinker the Second Logos and the Doer the Third Logos.

The Word is symbolized by a circle in which are a hexad of two interlaced triangles, and the point in the center. The point is the M, the triangle Aries, Leo, Sagittary is the A, the triangle Gemini, Libra, Aquarius is the U or the O, and the circle is the fully expressed point M as well as the line of the body I. The hexad is made up of the macrocosmic signs standing for the sexless triad and the androgynous triad, the triangle of God as Intelligence and the triangle of God as nature. These letters in which the perfect Self sounds, are symbolized in Masonry by the square and compass or the emblem of the interlaced triangles.

There is a succinct relationship of the Word with the Ineffable Name. The Word is feeling-and-desire, the Doer. The Doer is lost in the body of flesh and blood in the world of life and death. Thus the Doer is the *lost Word.* The body, when perfected, serves as the instrument through which the Doer pronounces the *Ineffable Name.* The *Ineffable Name* and the embodied *Word,* when one is fitted to speak it, is IAOM. By so doing the body is raised from a horizontal to an upright position.

The Name is pronounced as follows: It is started by opening the lips with an "ee" sound graduating into a broad "a" as the mouth opens wider with the lips forming an oval shape and then graduating the sound to "o" as the lips form a circle, and again modulating to an "m" sound as the lips close to a point. This point resolves itself to a point within the head.

Expressed phonetically the Name is "EE-Ah-Oh-Mmm" and is pronounced with one continuous outbreathing with a slight nasal tone in the manner described above. It can be correctly and properly expressed with its full power only by one who has brought his physical body to a state of perfection, that is, balanced and sexless.

SECTION 7

Summary of the teachings of Masonry. They center around "Light." The symbols, acts and words of the ritual. Ritualists and their workings. The permanent forms of Masonry and twisted teachings. Scriptural passages. Geometrical symbols. Their value. Masonry has in trust certain geometrical symbols which, coordinated in a system for the Masonic work, are thus preserved.

THE TEACHINGS of Masonry are few and definite. They are of the Supreme Intelligence, of the Light of the original state of the Triune Self, of the first body when the Doer was without sin and the body lived in the Light, of the death of the body, which is called the destruction of the temple, of the duty to rebuild the temple, of the training of the Doer of feeling-and-desire, as the candidate, to be conscious of itself in the body and to come into conscious relation with the Thinker and the Knower, which training is symbolized by the degrees of the Entered Apprentice, the Fellow Craft and the Master Mason, that is, the three parts of the Triune Self, of the sex power, called Hiram Abiff, by which the temple is rebuilt or the body made immortal, and of the Light filling the temple. The Masonic teachings center around the Light, the Conscious Light the Doer had, the Light it had lost and the Light it must regain. "More light" is the true Masonic prayer. Getting light is the phrase used in Masonry for becoming conscious in higher degrees. Masons take their obligations of virtue and holiness to get more light, to become children of Light.

The symbols, the symbolic acts and the words of the ritual do not always present these teachings. In the course of time and with the popularization of Masonry, some of these teachings have become obscured because of twisting, substituting and adding symbols and work. Various ritualists have been active, not always within the bounds or along the lines of the Masonic landmarks. Nevertheless, the fundamental forms remain, and show the misfits. The Doer, Thinker, and Knower parts are symbolized by the Junior Warden, Senior Warden, and Worshipful Master, by Jubela, Jubelo, and Jubelum, by the Entered Apprentice, the Fellow Craft, and the Master Mason, by Hiram Abiff, Hiram, King of Tyre, and King Solomon, by the Pillars of Beauty, Strength, and Wisdom. Where the same three parts are symbolized and there is an omission, it is clear that the later ritualists worked without understanding the relation of the three parts of the Triune Self. So the sun and the moon stand for the body and the feeling, but there is nothing for the desire in this imagery unless it be the stars, and in their place the ritual for the Entered Apprentice degree mentions the Master of the Lodge. Desire should be the Master of the Lodge in that degree. Boaz symbolizes the Thinker and Jachin the Knower, but there is nothing in the ritual to stand for the balancer, the Doer, which makes the arch below, corresponding to the Royal Arch above. However, notwithstanding twists, missing links and the use of the same symbol to indicate different subjects, the general forms of Masonry remain as guides, to which the growth of rites, orders and symbology is reduced from time to time.

Among the permanent forms of Masonry are the point in the circle, the oblong square or the form of the lodge, the right-angled triangle or the square, the equilateral triangle which is the symbol of the Supreme Intelligence, the compass as the symbol of the light coming down, the interlaced triangles, the two columns, the three Great Lights, the arch, the keystone with the two crosses, the white lambskin or apron, the cable-tow, the four degrees and the Master Builder. At such times much stress is laid on some of these symbols, at other times symbols like the trestle-board, the G or point in the circle, the All-seeing Eye as the symbol of the Supreme Intelligence, the source of all Light, and the Blazing Star, symbol of the teacher of the Messianic cycle, are made less important according to the understanding and fancy of the ritualists. Notwithstanding the warning against any change or removal of the ancient landmarks, Masons vary the ritual. Thus many of the teachings have become twisted. For instance, the fire which is a symbol of Jehovah is identified with the Light, which is representative of the Supreme Intelligence; the cardinal point, the North, through which the Light comes, has disappeared from the ritual and the North is dark; the Word is confounded with the Name; the explanation why the three officers act as three ruffians has disappeared.

Much of this deterioration is due to the fact that Scriptural passages which are parts of the ritual, are interpreted according to the religious sentiment of the times, and so color, distort or hide the Masonic teachings which the symbols preserve.

Masons have long been in a time of darkness. They are perhaps to be excused for the loss of the light in a time of general darkness. In the present age, however, if they are traveling in search of light, if light is the object of their search, they can find it by searching for it through their symbols. They will get more light if they try to hold the Conscious Light in thinking steadily on the meaning of their symbols.

A geometrical symbol expresses an idea and is a prototype for thinking. It is the original pattern after which other things are modeled, by which they are prefigured, predetermined and given identity, to which they correspond and to which they respond. All things can be epitomized and placed under a few prototypes from which they have originated and by which they are predetermined. Therefore, physical things can be summarized under abstractions which are symbolic. Symbols show a unity in diversity.

Many things can be used as symbols, but geometrical symbols are the highest, because they are best adapted to convey the idea that is expressed in them. The reason is that the body-mind, feeling-mind, and desire-mind work with points, lines, angles and curves, that geometrical forms are the simplest, the most direct and freest from irregularities and complications, and that, therefore, the functions of the three minds are at home with geometrical symbols and get from them without color, form, prejudice, variations and coverings, the essence in the idea or thought which the symbols convey. Points and lines are not seen on the physical plane. Matter on the physical plane appears in forms. These forms have outlines, that is, they end. Lines are conceptions, due to the functions of the feeling-mind and have no physical, tangible existence. They exist on the life plane of the physical world. Points and lines are the matter on the life plane, that is, if the matter on this plane could be seen or conceived, it would be to the average human understanding as points, lines, angles and curves. With this kind of matter, that is, points, lines, angles and curves, the body-mind can work. In order to get the meaning of anything that is not physical the body-mind thinks in points and lines.

A geometrical symbol is not colored, but everything in the world that is seen is colored and therefore does not show the truth, which is without color. True form is without color. Geometrical symbols are true forms. They show the actual character of the things they represent. The reason people cannot use geometrical symbols is that they are looking at the colored forms of nature and have to grow accustomed to geometrical symbols before they can use them and see through them. They first suggest and then reveal the idea they express. When a human thinks intentionally through geometrical symbols he can get the truth which the symbols contain.

All geometrical symbols have their origin in points, lines, angles and curves which receive their value as symbols from positions they hold in the circle. The

Zodiac is the best symbol of the circle with the twelve points on the circumference which give a value to geometrical symbols. The value which the symbols so receive is given them by their position relative to the twelve points. Masonry has its symbols from the Zodiac.

The chief reason Masonry exists, and has been preserved when other secret bodies have perished, is that it has in trust certain symbols and that these are coordinated and vitalized in a system for Masonic work. These symbols are geometrical. If Masonic symbols are tools, emblems or buildings, they are valuable because of the geometrical lines they embody.

———

Masons who have read the foregoing approved it, and it is now published with the hope that all readers will see its application to "The Great Way" described in *Thinking and Destiny,* and which preceded this work in the original manuscript. It is addressed to all human beings, and the author, though not a member of the Masonic Fraternity, wishes especially to remind all Masons, of whatever Lodge or Rite, that entrusted to their care were the plans for the rebuilding of their second temple which will be greater than the first temple that they destroyed in the long-ago-at-the-beginning of time.

The information for the building of an immortal physical body has been a closely guarded secret preserved through all the ages by the Masonic Fraternity. The works of the author are for the purpose of showing every human being, regardless of race, creed, or color, who really desires to return to and re-establish his Father's house in The Realm of Permanence may begin the Great Work without being crushed by the weight of the world's thought. That is to say, without having to leave his active work and retire from the world to do it in secret.

It is possible, but not probable, that human beings can rebuild their temples in the present life. However, anyone may prepare himself and become an entered apprentice and take as many degrees as he can in the present life and continue the work in the next life on earth.

This article also is to remind all Masons that it is *their work*. Let those, who will, see.

INDEX

Oblong square. The —, 53

Pledge. The —, 9
Point and the Circle, The —, 21
Preliminaries. Meaning of the —, 7
Preparations in the heart and for Initiation, 7
Principles of the three degrees. Fundamental —, 4

Ritual. The —, 52
Royal Arch. The —, 42
Ruffians. The finding of the three —, 29

Secret language. The —, 5
Signs and their meanings, 13
Signs, grips and words, 11
Solar germ. The —, 39
Solomon's Temple. King —, 14, 19, 21, 32
South gate, The —, 28
Stéps. The 3, 5, and 7 —, 19
Symbols. What the candidate learns about the —, 3, 10

Symbols and ceremonies. Purpose of the —, 15

Tabernacle. The —, 45
Temple. The second —, 3, 57
Thinking. Passive and active —, 5
Travels, 9
Trestle-board. The designs on the —, 28
Tools. The working —, 12
Triangles, 28, 32
Truths, locked up in trivial forms. Great —, 4
Twelve. The —, 32

Upright man. The Mason as an —, 12

Wages and Jewels. The —, 21
Word. The —, 14, 29
Workmen. The fifteen —, 32

Zodiac. The twelve points of the —, 32
Zodiacal signs. The —, 22

AFTERWORD

The title of *Masonry and Its Symbols* is qualified by the words "in the Light of *Thinking and Destiny,*" a monumental book published in 1946 after 34 years of profound preparation. In the Preface here, the author relates how a chapter on Freemasonry was withdrawn before *Thinking and Destiny* was published, and in order to help the reader understand this subsequently published book on Masonry, author Percival explains concepts and defines terms from *Thinking and Destiny.*

After having read *Masonry and Its Symbols,* you undoubtedly will want to seek more information from the same source in *Thinking and Destiny.* You are, therefore, invited to inquire about a special offer. Write to:

The Word Foundation, Inc.
P.O. Box 18235
Dallas, Texas 75218
U.S.A.

The succeeding pages tell, in part, what *Thinking and Destiny* contains and what it can do for you.

THINKING AND DESTINY

by Harold Waldwin Percival

1021 pages of text and foreword, including 30 pages of symbols, illustrations and charts, 31 pages of definitions and explanations, and an 11-page comprehensive index.

No single work reveals so clearly and so much on Man, his origin, progression, and ultimate destiny. This unique book . . .

. . . **Explains the Purpose** of life; What and where you are; Nature of the Soul; Consciousness; What happens at and after death.

. . . **Tells how thoughts** are created and exteriorized as objects, acts, and events in lives of individuals and collectively.

. . . **Discloses how you** alone control your life by your thinking which not only can change your Destiny, but your body, too.

. . . **Teaches the steps** that you and everyone must sooner or later take on the Great Way of Regeneration and Redemption.

Partial List of Subjects from the Table of Contents

PURPOSE AND PLAN OF THE UNIVERSE
Theories about the Soul. An accident is part of a thought. The wrath of God. Innate faith in justice. Story of Original Sin.

OPERATION OF THE LAW OF THOUGHT AS DESTINY
A thought is a being. How thoughts are created. Physical, psychic, mental, and noetic results of thoughts. Power of a thought. Hastening or delaying destiny. Responsibility. Conscience. Sin.

PHYSICAL DESTINY
Circumstances at birth. Healthy or sickly bodies. Unjust persecutions. Errors of justice. Span of life. Manner of death. Money. Poverty. Reversals. Wealth or inheritance is no accident. Rise and fall of nations. Agents of the Law. Priests. Gods. Intelligences govern order of events.

PSYCHIC DESTINY
Prenatal influences. Conception. Inheritance of former thoughts. First years of life. Mediumship. Materializations. Seances. Clairvoyance. Psychic powers. Vibrations. Colors. Astrology. Demon alcohol. Dreams. Nightmares. Hypnosis. Process of dying. To be conscious at death. States after death. Communications with the dead. Awareness that the body has died. Judgment. Hell is made by desires. The devil. Heaven is a reality.

MENTAL DESTINY
The Triune Self. An intelligence. Active, passive, real thinking. Morality of thinking. Sense-knowledge and self-knowledge. Honest thinking. Dishonest thinking. Responsibility and duty. Intuition. Genius. Realm of Permanence. Trial test of the sexes. Fall of Man. Wise men. Cycles and rise of the latest. Our age of thought. Mysticism. Spiritism. Mental healing. Thoughts are seeds of disease. Purpose of disease. Real cure. No escape from payment. Faith. Mesmerism. Self-hypnosis. Self-suggestion.
Ancient knowledge. Eastern movement. Pranayama, its dangers. System of Pantanjali, his eight steps of yoga. Meaning of Sanscrit. Traces of ancient teaching. What the West wants. States of a human in deep sleep, in trance. Twelve stages between re-existences. Mental hells and heavens.

THE POINT OR CIRCLE

Creation of a thought, method of thinking. Thinking without creating destiny. Pre-chemistry. Dimensions. Heavenly bodies. Time, Space.

THE CIRCLE OR ZODIAC

The Twelve Nameless Points. Symbolism and value of the Zodiac. How it reveals the purpose of the Universe. As a record of history and prophecy.

THINKING: THE WAY TO CONSCIOUS IMMORTALITY

For whom this system of thinking is presented. Becoming conscious of Consciousness. Stages on The Way to Conscious Immortality.